I0772343

# MOTORCYCLES
## A GUIDE TO THE WORLD'S BEST BIKES™

# DUCATI
## HIGH-PERFORMANCE ITALIAN RACER

rosen publishing's
rosen central®

NEW YORK

RICHARD BARRINGTON

Published in 2014 by The Rosen Publishing Group, Inc.
29 East 21st Street, New York, NY 10010

First Edition

**Library of Congress Cataloging-in-Publication Data**

Barrington, Richard, 1961–
Ducati: high-performance Italian racer/Richard Barrington.
    pages cm.—(Motorcycles: A Guide to the World's Best Bikes)
Audience: Grade 5 to 8.
Includes bibliographical references and index.
ISBN 978-1-4777-1856-8 (library binding)—
ISBN 978-1-4777-1870-4 (paperback)—
ISBN 978-1-4777-1871-1 (6-pack)
1. Ducati motorcycle—Juvenile literature. I. Title.
TL448.D8B37 2014
629.227'5—dc23

                                                    2013013201

*Manufactured in the United States of America*

CPSIA Compliance Information: Batch #W14YA: For further information, contact Rosen Publishing, New York, New York, at 1-800-237-9932.

# CONTENTS

Ducati may not quite be a household name in North America, but to motorcycle enthusiasts around the world, it is a name that will bring a knowing nod of respect or a smile of appreciation. The Italian company's bikes are sold in sixty countries around the world, where Ducatis have distinguished themselves on racetracks and on public roads, both paved and unpaved.

Ducati originally established itself as a manufacturer of radio equipment, not motorcycles. When it did get into building motorcycles after World War II, it started small, very small. Its first product along these lines was a small motor designed to be attached as an add-on to bicycles. Soon after, Ducati began building its own frames for these motors. By the 1950s, the company had a lineup of multiple motorcycles, and it began to build a reputation for high performance that continues to this day.

What's special about Ducati? The uniqueness starts from the outside in. Motorcycle design is often copied from one company to another, with manufacturers sticking to established formulas or perhaps trying to imitate a handful of the most popular bikes.

Its racing success is just one element of Ducati's reputation for excellence.
Here is Valentino Rossi qualifying for a recent MotoGP race.

Ducati bikes, on the other hand, don't look quite like anything else. Their bodywork is generally kept to a minimum, though with the distinctly Italian flair of these bikes' design details, the overall effect is stylish rather than severe.

Ducati bikes also go their own way when it comes to market categories. Though Ducati builds machines that compete in popular segments, such as touring bikes, cruisers, and off-road or enduro bikes, Ducati's take on these categories often incorporates elements of other categories as well, giving the brand less of a cookie-cutter lineup than most manufacturers.

Ducati has backed up its style with true substance in the form of a proud track record in motorcycle racing. It has won over a dozen driver's and manufacturer's titles in Superbike racing and has also seen success in MotoGP racing. Still, one doesn't have to be a racer to appreciate Ducati's bikes. The examples highlighted in this resource, which are just a part of the full Ducati lineup, will help demonstrate why Ducatis are considered bikes for true motorcycle enthusiasts.

# THE DIAVEL: A CRUISER WITH AN EDGE

**D**iavel is the Italian word for "devil," which helps explain the fierce look of Ducati's Diavel motorcycle. Though generally classified as a cruiser, this bike bends the category, demanding some kind of description added to the category, such as "sport cruiser" or "power cruiser."

Cruisers, after all, are the most classic category of motorcycle. They are usually modeled with a healthy dose of nostalgia for old-time American bike design. With the Diavel, though, the nostalgia doesn't make it any farther than the front headlight. The Diavel does have the single, round headlight typical of cruisers, but beyond that, everything else on the bike is more modern and sporty than one would expect from a cruiser.

The instrument panel and rear mirrors are stylishly aerodynamic and jet black rather than the conventional chrome. The fuel tank gives the front end of the bike the wide bearing of a cruiser, but the air intakes mounted along the sides of that tank also lend the Diavel the hungry look of a fighter plane. Beneath the fuel tank, an exposed tubular frame adds a signature Ducati design element to the Diavel.

From there to the back of the bike, the Diavel really abandons any cruiser bike elements and looks much more

The Diavel brings aerodynamic sport bike elements to the classic cruiser and is available in a number of trim packages, including the Cromo version shown here.

like a sport bike. The saddle is somewhat unconventional, looking almost like a miniature bucket seat. Meanwhile, the upswept tail and exhaust mufflers complete the sporty impression of the back half of the bike.

This is not a bike for anyone who wants classic cruiser styling, but it would be a compelling choice for someone who's looking for a bike that can announce itself as something different—even before the engine is started.

# CAN'T DECIDE BETWEEN A CRUISER AND A SPORT BIKE?

Motorcycle enthusiasts fantasize about owning a fleet of different bikes, each fulfilling a distinct role or just scratching a different itch. The financial reality is that the typical bike owner has to make do with just one machine.

The gut-wrenching question, then, becomes "Which bike?" It's a tough enough decision given the number of brands and models that are available, but riders may also struggle with choosing what category of bike they want to own. For example: cruiser or sport bike? Does the rider want a comfortable, upright sitting position for long rides, a passenger-friendly back seat, and low-slung, classic styling? That would suggest a cruiser. On the other hand, if acceleration and handling are priorities, along with more of a high-tech image, then a sport bike might be the right choice.

To some extent, the Ducati Diavel might answer both needs. It has the low seat and throaty rumble of a cruiser, but the initial burst and light weight of a sport bike. Riders looking for a bike to fill both roles might especially want to consider the Diavel Strada. This design package retains the sporty profile of the basic Diavel but has a few more cruiser-like features, such as side bags, a padded rear seat with a sissy bar, and raised handlebars.

Ducatis don't come cheap, so the Diavel isn't a low-budget way into either the cruiser or the sport bike market. However, as an alternative to owning both a cruiser and a sport bike, getting elements of both from a Diavel might be an economical decision.

# Elements of Power

Ducati likens the Diavel to a well-proportioned athlete, and that description really hits home when comparing the bike's power with its size. A 1,200 cubic centimeter (73.2 cubic inch) twin-cylinder engine is fairly standard stuff for a cruiser, but an engine that size won't typically be found in a bike with a dry weight of just 463 pounds (210 kilograms). This gives the Ducati its athletic characteristics, with an engine capable of generating 162 horsepower housed in a fairly small frame.

To keep the Diavel's dimensions so trim, Ducati has equipped the bike with a modestly sized 4.5-gallon (17-liter) gas tank, so cruising range will be more limited than for some bikes in the class. What's not so modestly sized is the Diavel's unusually wide rear tire, which is not something one would expect on a classic cruiser.

A wide rear tire and antilock brakes are among the enhanced performance features Ducati has brought to its Diavel cruiser.

A six-speed gearbox gives riders hands-on control over the acceleration curve. Control freaks will also like the fact that the Diavel lets you choose from among three different riding modes. This feature tailors performance characteristics according to whether you are in sport, touring, or urban riding conditions.

As for looks, the base model of the Diavel comes in bright blue or red, but there are five other styling packages, which give riders the option of expressing their individual preferences. These styling packages often feature an appropriately sinister amount of black, for those who want to further enhance this bike's devilish image.

## Superior Performance

The technical characteristics of a bike are all well and good on paper, but the real test is whether they translate into performance on the road. Most reviewers seem to agree that the Ducati Diavel passes this test with flying colors.

While the Diavel has the feet-forward riding position of a classic cruiser, its deep and sharply curved seat makes that position less relaxed than is usual for this class of bike. The reason for that less-relaxed riding position becomes apparent once the bike is in motion.

The crisp rumble of the Ducati's engine will satisfy anyone who feels that a cruiser's bark should at least match its bite, but the Ducati can back up its talk with action. The Diavel is both quick off the line and quick to stop. The engine may have less horsepower than some in the cruiser class, but when powering

The Ducati Diavel's 1,200 cubic centimeter (73.2 cubic inch) engine delivers 162 horsepower to a relatively lightweight frame, giving the bike impressive acceleration.

this relatively light machine it delivers impressive acceleration. Traction control helps the bike to handle well on twisty roads despite the fat rear tire and long, 62.6-inch (1,590-millimeter) wheelbase. Antilock brakes bring all that power under control with a suddenness that can seem abrupt until the rider gets used to it.

The Diavel has been praised as a real breakthrough in the cruiser category, a next-generation type of bike, which won *Cycle World* magazine's Best Cruiser category in its first two years of availability.

# CHAPTER TWO

## HYPERMOTARD: SLEEK MEETS GEEK

There is a gangly, almost awkward look to dirt bikes. They are a bit like a teenager who has just had a growth spurt—tall and thin in a spindly sort of way. Of course, they are built that way for a reason. The height gives them the ground clearance and fork travel necessary for off-road riding. Their thinness makes them light and easy to handle or even pick up after an occasional spill. Finally, their lack of emphasis on aerodynamics gives the rider a straight up-and-down position suited for maximum control.

Considering all this, it is difficult to believe that the design for Ducati's Hypermotard began with the concept of a dirt bike. The sharply angled front, V-shaped headlight, and stylish black accents help the Hypermotard make a refined, sophisticated first impression. Look more closely, though, and some dirt-bike elements are still apparent. Extended forks lift the bike up fairly high, and the bike is designed for the rider to sit tall in the saddle. Hand guards protect the grip on the handlebars. The overall appearance is lean enough for Ducati's signature tubular chassis to be partially exposed.

The Hypermotard, then, is a dirt bike all grown up, with some polish and sophistication, but still enough of that youthful athleticism to handle some rough terrain. In short, this bike is

The Hypermotard has the high ground clearance of a dirt bike, but its angular design elements add a distinctly stylish flair.

another category bender from Ducati, a bike that can satisfy more than one type of need.

## Details and Options

One way to look at the technical specifications of the Hypermotard is to break them down between those that are consistent with its dirt-bike design roots, and those that represent a departure from that background.

# URBAN COWBOY

City streets and dirt roads: they are usually literally miles apart and occupy opposite ends of the spectrum in terms of the surroundings that riders may find themselves in. And yet, even with its dirt-bike design origins, the Hypermotard is curiously well suited for an urban environment.

Take road surfaces, for example. Instead of rutted dirt roads, the urban rider might encounter cavernous potholes or even nineteenth-century cobblestones. In either case, the Hypermotard's high stance and forgiving suspension can help smooth out the bumps. The straight up-and-down riding position is ideal for the frequent stops one has to make in the city. The light weight will help with street parking maneuvers, while the skinny profile is ideal for snaking through tight spaces.

The Hypermotard is certainly more versatile than a purely urban mode of transportation, but for riders who spend a fair amount of time in the city, its toughness and agility may make it a good choice for the mean streets. While a classic dirt bike would look awkward in an urban setting, the Hypermotard's chic European styling gives it form and function.

The most apparent physical similarity between the Hypermotard and a traditional dirt bike is high clearance between the tires and their fenders. This allows a generous 6.7 inches (170 mm) of fork travel for the front wheel, and 5.9 inches (150 mm) for the rear. The SP version of the Hypermotard allows for even

In addition to introducing style to a dirt bike frame, the Hypermotard also includes a twin-cylinder engine rather than the ordinary dirt bike's single cylinder.

greater shock absorption, with 7.3 inches (185 mm) of travel in front and 6.9 inches (175 mm) in back. On all versions, the hand guards are another nod to the off-road tradition, though their rich black finish and integrated turn signals suggest they are not really for heavy-duty use.

Sleek styling is just one way the Hypermotard departs from the dirt bike category. Perhaps most important is the engine, where a sophisticated L-twin replaces the typical single-cylinder power plant. In part because of that additional cylinder, engine displacement exceeds 800 cubic centimeters (48.8 cubic inches), much larger than the motor on a normal dirt bike. Also, the Hypermotard's highly sophisticated digital instrument panel produces details such as air temperature and average fuel consumption, things that would not typically be of immediate concern to a dirt biker.

The result of this dirt bike/street bike hybrid is a dry weight that falls somewhere between the two categories at 386 pounds (175 kg). This is still light enough for the average rider to set the bike back upright with ease. Yet, the Hypermotard's sleek finish will make the rider want to avoid dropping the bike in the first place.

## A Rough Rider with Manners

Technically, the Hypermotard has elements that are like a dirt bike, but also those that are a clear departure.

While the high stance and ample amount of fork travel make this bike competent on rough terrain, certain design choices indicate that it was primarily intended for pavement. Having a two-cylinder rather than a one-cylinder engine gives it a stronger and steadier source of power, and the styling is certainly more refined than the plastic Day-Glo look common to pure dirt bikes. The one drawback of this split personality is that having so much give in the suspension has been reported to make the bike feel a little unsettled on the open road, though not so much as to affect handling once the rider is used to the sensation.

While the Hypermotard has the high stance of a dirt bike, its engine size and horsepower make it well suited to paved roads.

By keeping the weight down while installing a sizeable engine, Ducati has given the Hypermotard an impressive amount of speed. While the Hypermotard's build will help it slog through some rough footing, producing 110 hp on a light frame will also allow the bike to move swiftly along the open road. The ability to select riding modes for sport, touring, or urban conditions helps ensure that whatever the terrain, the Hypermotard will handle it gracefully.

# CHAPTER THREE

# THE MONSTER: A BEAUTY OF A BEAST

**W**hether it's a matter of technology or styling, motorcycle design has fashions that come and go. The risk of buying something that is cutting-edge today is that the fashions of the moment often are the most dated looking styles in five or ten years.

In contrast, Ducati's Monster is a bike that has stood the test of time. This model has been around for over twenty years, and over 250,000 of them have been sold. Something with such widespread and long-lasting popularity deserves to be considered a classic.

At first glance, the Monster looks a fair amount like a European take on a traditional American bike. Upon closer examination, though, the more rearward placement of the foot pegs and the relatively low handlebars are clearly intended to put the rider in more of a sport bike position. The narrow seat and sharp upward angle of the bike's tail and mufflers add to the sporty impression.

Like the Diavel, this bike may belong somewhere between the cruiser and sport bike categories, though the Monster is even leaner and more stripped down than the Diavel. A focal point of the bike is the exposed tubular chassis frame, a signature that makes it clear that while its category may be hard to define, this bike is definitely a Ducati.

The Monster's tubular frame has been a signature design element throughout its long history, even as new technological refinements have been added.

## Raw Power

There are six different versions of the Monster but essentially three engine sizes: a 696 cubic centimeter (42.5 cubic inch), a 796 cubic centimeter (48.6 cubic inch), and an 1,100 cubic centimeter (67.1 cubic inch). As is the habit with motorcycle manufacturers, the displacement sizes they use to label their models are approximations; the actual displacement statistics can be found in the table at the end of this resource.

# *THE TWENTIETH ANNIVERSARY VERSION*

Having a model survive twenty years is certainly worthy of celebration, and for 2013 Ducati introduced a special twentieth anniversary version of the Monster to mark that milestone.

One reason for the Monster's staying power is its classic styling. Flipping through a photo gallery of Monsters from over the past twenty years shows that aside from a few refinements here and there, the basic look of the bike has remained unchanged over its lifetime. The company has moved with the times in terms of using technological advancements and introducing different engine sizes, but the basic character of the bike is the same now as it was in 1993.

Ducati promotes the fact that Monster owners like to customize the bike, and in some ways the naked styling is the ideal blank canvas on which a rider can leave a personal mark. For the twentieth anniversary version, though, Ducati has done some customizing of its own. The most obvious of these special features is the bold bronze coloring of the front fork and frame. Subtler touches include a vintage tank decal and gold brake housings. This celebration of a classic is something that any bike lover might well enjoy checking out.

What the three sizes of Monsters have in common are L-twin, air-cooled engines, with 6-speed transmissions. Antilock braking is standard on the 1100 and optional on the 696 and 796. The most significant characteristic these versions share is a stripped-down form of styling popularly known as "naked."

The practical result of this bare-bones design is that even though none of the engines deliver an extraordinary amount of horsepower, each bike gets the most out of its power because it is driving a relatively lightweight machine. The proportion of horsepower to weight ranges from 80 horsepower at a dry weight of 355 pounds (161 kg) for the standard 696 model, to 100 horsepower at a dry weight of 373 pounds (169 kg) for the 1100.

The Ducati Monster features an air-cooled, L-twin engine that delivers a fair amount of power to this stylish machine.

The no-frills, naked styling of the Monster has helped give the design staying power over the years, while it also means that there is no excess weight to bog the bike down. The result is that whether it's the 696, the 796, or the 1100, each engine can deliver pure power.

## No-Nonsense Performance

The no-nonsense appearance of the Monster translates to the bike's performance, which is more about responsiveness and handling than it is about comfort and smoothness.

The engine makes its presence felt in volume and vibration,

While stunts like wheelies should be left to professional riders, the torque the Monster produces will be appreciated in more routine acceleration as well.

which will be a positive for some riders and not for others. The Monster is not particularly happy in stop-and-go traffic, as the clutch is so responsive that the bike has a tendency to lurch forward when power is engaged. However, that same responsiveness is a plus when it's time to accelerate onto the highway, as the Monster can get up to speed with ease.

Once at highway speeds, the ride is far from cushy, but on twisty roads that same firmness will give the bike a sure-footed feel. One drawback for a bike that is so at home moving at speed on the open road is that gas tank volume is limited. For versions of the Monster with antilock brakes, the tank will hold just 3.6 gallons (13.5 liters), thus limiting cruising range.

There are plenty of bikes that are designed to cushion the rider against some of the harsher realities of torque, engine vibration, and rough road surfaces. In contrast, the Monster is true to its no-frills styling, delivering the immediate and intuitive feel of no-nonsense performance.

# CHAPTER FOUR

## MULTISTRADA: A BIKE WITH MULTIPLE PERSONALITIES

**W**hile Ducatis generally tend to be category benders, that versatility is perhaps most evident in the Multistrada 1200. The "multi" in the name refers to the multiple roles Ducati sees this bike as playing—enduro, urban, touring, and sport. Ducati enables this by giving the rider a choice of four riding modes, which can be selected on the fly to fit the situation. Those riding modes adjust the power delivery of the engine, the traction control, and the antilock braking system. On some versions of the Multistrada they even adjust the suspension.

For a bike with all of this going on, the Multistrada does not look especially unusual. There are some elements that instantly identify the bike as a Ducati: the sharply pointed front, the stylishly angular lights and mirrors, and the partially exposed tubular frame, though that frame is somewhat less prominent than on other models.

Overall, the first impression the bike creates is of a modestly sized touring bike. On closer examination though, there are some features that don't fit that first impression. The suspension jacks the bike up above the tires higher than usual for a touring bike, a nod to the enduro side of the Multistrada's personality. A set of hand guards reinforces the enduro characteristics. The tail is tapered and swept upward, in a style that is more like a sport than a touring bike. In short, the Multistrada wears its multiple personalities on its sleeve. Ducatis, after all, don't like to be categorized.

## A Wealth of Features

To pull off the four-bikes-in-one concept of the Multistrada, Ducati has packed it with technical features. In addition to the antilock brakes, traction control, and choice of four riding modes, the Multistrada has an instrument panel with a

With a look that is part enduro, part sport, and part touring bike, the Multistrada's various personalities are on full display.

range of details one might expect to find on the dashboard of a luxury car rather than on a motorcycle.

Surprisingly, while blending the elements of four bikes into one and providing so many high-end features, Ducati has kept the Multistrada's dry weight down to a reasonable 423 pounds (196 kg). Driving that weight is a liquid-cooled 1,200 cubic centimeter (73.2 cubic inch) engine, which delivers an impressive 150 horsepower via a six-speed transmission.

The Multistrada comes in four different versions: a base 1200 model, and three "S" versions that include the Skyhook suspension system. This system incorporates feedback from the engine, brakes, and road conditions to automatically adjust the suspension setup. Two of the S versions are touring models, while the Pikes Peak version is clad in an enduro-style paint scheme. The latter name is not just for show; the Multistrada has won multiple Pikes Peak hill climbs, evidence that the bike packs some power behind its various personalities.

## Touring in Style

Ultimately, even with its sport and enduro elements, the Multistrada is primarily a touring bike. Touring is such a large category that it has spawned subcategories, such as sport touring and adventure touring, and the Multistrada fits somewhere in this modified area of the touring category. It is smaller in engine size and weight than the huge touring bikes that are built primarily for long-distance comfort, and this makes the Multistrada more versatile.

# HOW MUCH BIKE?

Motorcycle riders typically start out on small, simple bikes, and then work their way up to bigger and fancier machines. At some point in this evolution, they face a key decision: how much bike do they need?

Motorcycles, after all, can come with 1,800 cubic centimeter (109.8 cubic inch) engines and weigh around a 1,000 pounds (453 kg). However, sometimes riders who work their way up to that kind of behemoth find themselves missing the ease and unfiltered riding experience of a more moderately sized machine.

For riders who are experienced with mid-sized bikes and want something more, the Ducati Multistrada might be a good way of taking the next step without going too far. Its 1,200 cubic centimeter (73.2 cubic inch) engine definitely puts it toward the big bike end of the spectrum, but its clean profile and relatively light weight don't isolate the rider from a pure motorcycling experience. Furthermore, the versatility of the Multistrada might represent a good solution for riders who don't want to get pigeonholed into one type of bike.

Ultimately, bikers who want to specialize in one type of riding—whether it's touring, sport biking, or off-road—would be best served by choosing a specialist bike in their favorite category. However, bikers who plan on a range of biking experiences might well prefer the Multistrada, a bike that can multitask and do it effectively.

At the same time, the Multistrada does not sacrifice comfort, though the 33.5-inch (850-mm) seat height might be challenging to shorter riders. The seat is comfortably slim, and the windscreen can be adjusted with one hand even while the bike is in motion, so the rider can choose a level of protection from the elements suitable for speed and conditions.

The multiple riding modes help bring out the best in the Multistrada based on the situation. For example, power delivery is smooth and not too overeager in the urban mode but can also provide more immediate torque in the sport mode.

The Multistrada's versatility makes it an ideal choice for riders who want to have a range of different riding experiences with one bike.

Between those two extremes, the touring mode delivers good all-around performance.

The traction control system also helps the Multistrada adapt to conditions. This feature helps make city stop-and-go driving less herky-jerky and also eases power delivery on wet roads to reduce tire spin.

While it's doubtful one would actually want to spend much time off road with a bike this big and this expensive, the enduro characteristics of the bike should help it navigate the occasional dirt road. Overall, this is a touring bike that allows the rider to apply a broad definition to where touring can lead.

# CHAPTER FIVE

# STREETFIGHTER: NAKED AGGRESSION

**D**ucati announced its intentions for this bike pretty bluntly by naming it the Streetfighter. This is a bike built to earn street credibility, and physically it is stripped down to pack a punch. In fact, the Streetfighter is so stripped down that it looks almost like an anatomical model of a motorcycle, with the outside peeled back to show how things work inside. Instead of ribs, there is the tubular steel frame holding everything firmly in place; instead of a beating heart, there is the 849 cubic centimeter (51.8 cubic inch) engine; instead of lungs, there are the forward-mounted radiator and large air intake.

Although the Streetfighter comes in three colors—red, black, or yellow—these colors are just accents to the exposed workings of the bike because there is little in the way of superficial trim on this bike. Except for the gas tank cover, practically the only splashes of color are the minimalist front fender and a back seat that tapers to a point as it rises high above the rear wheel.

To anyone who loves motorcycles, this scarcity of design elements makes the bike anything but plain. With so much exposed, the Ducati is simply all about the machine—and to many, that's a beautiful thing.

## Pound-for-Pound Power

In the boxing world, fighters are divided into weight divisions, to acknowledge the fact that bigger fighters are likely to be stronger. However, to compare fighters across weight classes, boxing fans refer to who is the best pound-for-pound—that is, who packs the most punch relative to his or her weight. In a similar way, the Streetfighter can be thought of as a pound-for-pound champion.

# HANDLING POWER RESPONSIBLY

Safety is always a good topic when discussing motorcycles, and it may be appropriate to bring it up in the context of describing a bike like the Streetfighter. It's not that the Streetfighter is an especially dangerous bike. As noted elsewhere in this section, the Streetfighter actually smooths out some of the harsher edges of sport bikes. Still, the Streetfighter's aggressive name and relatively affordable pricing might attract younger riders who are looking for their first truly powerful bike. It's important that those riders understand that with power comes responsibility. Here are some bike safety basics:

- Never ride after consuming drugs or alcohol.

- Do not street race or otherwise let other riders influence your behavior.

- Go easy when first carrying a passenger—stopping distances and cornering are affected with the added weight, and having someone else on the bike can be a distraction.

- When you view an obstacle in the road, focus on the safe route around the obstacle rather than on the obstacle itself. The bike tends to go in the direction the rider is looking.

  Younger riders may feel entitled to take risks with their own safety, but they should understand that the risks they take can endanger passengers, other riders, motorists, and pedestrians. Graduating to becoming a true biker includes knowing how to handle power responsibly.

The Streetfighter's 849 cubic centimeter (51.8 cubic inch) engine is smaller than the top-end option on any Ducati model except for the Hypermotard. A benefit of this is that the Streetfighter weighs a trim 373 pounds (169 kg) dry, while being capable of delivering 132 horsepower from its 4-valve L-twin engine. As usual for the Ducati line, the transmission is six-speed, and on the Streetfighter it is engaged via a wet multi-plate clutch.

In keeping with the bare-bones image of the Streetfighter, there is just one base model available in the United States (a larger, 1,099 cubic centimeter [67.1 cubic inch]

The bare-bones, naked styling of the Streetfighter emphasizes the mechanical components of the bike while helping to keep its weight down.

version is available in Europe), and unlike many of the other Ducati models, there is no antilock braking system, though the Brembo braking system should provide plenty of stopping bite in the hands of a competent rider.

## The Proof Is in the Performance

The Streetfighter borrows some components from Ducati's Superbike but represents a less extreme version of that pure racing machine. Thus, despite the aggressive name, the Streetfighter is actually a sporty bike with a practical side. It does not have all the technological bells and whistles of a high-end sport bike, but that gives it a more accessible price point.

The Streetfighter's engine delivers less peak power than a racing bike but is more comfortable at mid-range RPMs, so the engine does not have to be kept at extremely high revs in order to provide a decent amount of torque. At the same time, this engine is enough of a thoroughbred to be a little awkward at low revs, so this is not a bike for the low speeds and frequent stops of city driving.

By calming down some of the sport bike extremes and limiting the high-tech touches to keep cost and weight down, Ducati has produced something of a throwback bike. It even allows its traction-control system to be turned off for riders who want to go by pure feel. This bike won't have all the bells and whistles or peak performance of higher-end models, but for bikers looking for a more fundamental ride, the Streetfighter might be just the right fit.

# CHAPTER SIX

# SUPERBIKE 1199 PANIGALE: A RACING PEDIGREE

most models in the Ducati line tend to bend traditional categories by crossing over elements of more than one type of motorcycle. The Ducati Superbike 1199 Panigale, on the other hand, is a pure Superbike, which means that it belongs to the highest-powered class of commercially available racing motorcycles. Without a high degree of specialization, it would be impossible for a bike to compete at the highest level of international racing, so the Superbike 1199 Panigale can be thought of as a thoroughbred racer.

Aerodynamics are a priority for racing bikes, and on the 1199 Panigale this defines the look in a dramatic way. The front half of the bike is cloaked in a smooth sheath of bodywork, to allow air to flow over the bike with minimum resistance. The back seat is high and angled forward, and the handlebars are low and tucked neatly into the front fairing. This allows the rider to stretch forward to become part of the machine's aerodynamic shape.

Unlike most other Ducatis, the Superbikes do not have the exposed tubular frame. However, while that design element has been sacrificed for aerodynamics, the dramatic lines of this bike are still, as the company describes it, "distinctively Ducati."

A sweeping sheath of bodywork is both the most dramatic styling feature of the Ducati Panigale and a key to its aerodynamic performance.

# The High End of Power

Racing machines generally seek to find the best balance between power and weight. In designing the 1199 Panigale, Ducati was acutely aware of this key trade-off. The firm's goal was to improve their previous Superbike by adding 25 horsepower while cutting 10 kilograms (22 pounds) of weight.

The result is a 1198 cubic centimeter (73.1 cubic inch) L-twin engine that can deliver 195 horsepower to a machine

# THE RACER AS FLAGSHIP

Ducati puts a high level of ingenuity and engineering excellence into all its models. However, if it seems the technological standard of the 1199 Panigale is especially high, that shouldn't be a big surprise. There is a great deal at stake with a Superbike. Not only is the racing series extremely competitive, but results on the racetrack go a long way toward maintaining a manufacturer's reputation and attracting new customers.

The 1199 Panigale has a tough act to follow because even before its debut season, Ducati enjoyed a high level of racing success. In 2012, Ducati riders took three out of the top ten spots in the FIM Superbike World Championship standings.

Time will tell whether the 1199 Panigale can continue this high level of achievement. However, even before the 1199 Panigale joined the Superbike racing series, Motorcycle.com was impressed enough by the bike's potential to name it one of the "Top 10 Hottest Bikes of 2012." Anyone interested in a thoroughbred Superbike may want to check out the 1199 Panigale to see if they agree.

with a dry weight of just 361.5 pounds (164 kg). To make the most efficient use of every precious pound, Ducati has made the engine part of the structural support to the frame.

The six-speed gearbox is designed to provide maximum torque while not requiring the rider to provide an additional amount of force while shifting. Conventional disc brakes are given the task of bringing the 1199 Panigale under control, though an antilock braking system is available as an option. Ducati's technical specifications caution that the antilock brakes will add 5.5 pounds (2.5 kg) to the machine, though it is doubtful most riders will be as sensitive as racing teams are to the addition of that amount of weight.

The 1199 Panigale is available in four option packages, including the Pani-gale S, which comes with a race-ready mechanical setup. Ducati also makes a smaller Super-bike, the 848evo, which delivers 140 horsepower from its smaller engine.

## World-Class Performance

For a bike designed for premium per-formance, the 1199 Panigale is surpris-ingly comfortable. The seat is reason-ably low, and with a thin tail and centrally

The demands of high-level racing put the emphasis on efficient engineer-ing when developing engines for Superbikes such as the 1199 Panigale.

positioned tail pipe, there isn't much the rider has to swing a leg over. Compared to previous Ducati Superbikes, the 1199 Panigale's handlebars are a little higher and wider, and the seat position is slightly further forward. These tweaks make the riding position less extreme.

Like most high-performance bikes, the 1199 Panigale is designed to perform best at high revs. The wet clutch engages smoothly, and acceleration is even but unspectacular—at first. Speed begins to build more quickly north of 7,500 RPM, and torque and horsepower peak when revs exceed 9,000.

The light weight of the 1199 Panigale makes it very ready to lean into a turn, resulting in responsive handling. Braking is quite sensitive but doesn't lack for strength either. The antilock braking option may be a wise choice for riders who aren't quite used to the touchiness of race-caliber brakes.

The 1199 Panigale lets the rider choose from three riding modes—race, sport, and rain—depending on conditions. Race mode produces the most immediate and pronounced response to the controls.

A pure racing machine like the 1199 Panigale is a thoroughbred, and like a thoroughbred it demands a skilled and experienced rider. Everything on this type of bike will have heightened sensitivity—starting, stopping, turning, etc. The rider who can bring a subtle touch to all that sensitivity will get the most out of this bike.

# SPECIFICATIONS CHART

## DIAVEL

| | |
|---|---|
| displacement | 1198.4cc  /  73.1c/in |
| wheel base | 1,590mm  /  62.6in |
| horsepower | 162hp @ 9,500 rpm |
| torque | 94 lb/ft @ 8,000 rpm |
| transmission | 6 speed |
| fuel capacity | 4.5 gallons  /  17 liters |

## HYPERMOTARD

| | |
|---|---|
| displacement | 821.1cc  /  50.1c/in |
| wheel base | 1,500mm  /  59.1in |
| horsepower | 110hp @ 9,250 rpm |
| torque | 65.8 lb/ft @ 7,750 |
| transmission | 6 speed |
| fuel capacity | 4.2 gallons  /  16 liters |

## MONSTER

| | |
|---|---|
| displacement | 1078cc  /  65.8c/in |
| wheel base | 1,450mm  /  57.1in |
| horsepower | 100hp @ 7,500 rpm |
| torque | 76 lb/ft @ 6,000 rpm |
| transmission | 6 speed |
| fuel capacity | 3.6 gallons  /  13.5 liters |

## MULTISTRADA

| | |
|---|---|
| displacement | 1198.4cc  /  73.1c/in |
| wheel base | 1,530mm  /  60.2in |
| horsepower | 150hp @ 9,250 rpm |
| torque | 91.8 lb/ft @ 7,500 rpm |
| transmission | 6 speed |
| fuel capacity | 5.3 gallons  /  20 liters |

## STREETFIGHTER

| | |
|---|---|
| displacement | 849cc  / 51.8c/in |
| wheel base | 1,475mm  /  58.1in |
| horsepower | 132hp @ 10,000 rpm |
| torque | 69 lb/ft @ 9,500 |
| transmission | 6 speed |
| fuel capacity | 4.4 gallons  /  16.5 liters |

## 1199 PANIGALE

| | |
|---|---|
| displacement | 1198cc  /  73.1c/in |
| wheel base | 1,437mm  /  56.6 in |
| horsepower | 195hp @ 10,750 |
| torque | 98.1 lb/ft @ 9,000 |
| transmission | 6 speed |
| fuel capacity | 4.5 gallons  /  17 liters |

# FOR MORE INFORMATION

American Motorcyclist Association
13515 Yarmouth Drive
Pickerington, OH 43147
(800) 262-5646
Web site: http://www.americanmotorcyclist.com
The American Motorcyclist Association organizes motorcycle
  events and promotes the interests of motorcycle owners.

Canadian Motorcycle Association
605 James Street N., 4th Floor
Hamilton, ON L8L1J9
Canada
(905) 522-5705
Web site: http://www.canmocycle.ca
The Canadian Motorcycle Association is dedicated to promoting
  the interests of motorcycle riders in Canada.

Canadian Motosport Racing Corporation
P.O. Box 1466
Stouffville, ON L4A 8A3
Canada
(905) 642-5607
Web site: http://www.cmracing.com
The Canadian Motosport Racing Corporation is an organiza-
  tion that oversees off-road motorcycle racing in Canada.

Motorcycle Riders Foundation
236 Massachusetts Avenue NE, Suite 204
Washington, DC 20002

(202) 546-0983
Web site: http://www.mrf.org
The Motorcycle Riders Foundation is a not-for-profit organiza-
tion that advocates for the rights of motorcyclists.

Motorcycle Safety Foundation
2 Jenner Street, Suite 150
Irvine, CA 92618
(949) 727-3227
Web site: http://www.msf-usa.org
The Motorcycle Safety Foundation is a not-for-profit orga-
nization geared toward advancing rider education and
training.

US DESMO
P.O. Box 615
Waxhaw, NC 28179
(704) 843-0429
Web site: http://www.usdesmo.com
US DESMO is a club for Ducati owners in the United States.

# Web Sites

Due to the changing nature of Internet links, Rosen Publishing
has developed an online list of Web sites related to the subject
of this book. This site is updated regularly. Please use this link
to access the list:

http://www.rosenlinks.com/MOTO/Ducat

# FOR FURTHER READING

Aynsley, Phil. *Ducati a Photographic Tribute.* Sydney, New South Wales, Australia: Gti Media, 2010.

DK Publishing. *Motorcycle: The Definitive Visual History.* New York, NY: DK Publishing, 2012.

Falloon, Ian. *The Ducati Story, 5th Edition: Road and Racing Motorcycles from 1945 to the Present Day.* Sparkford, Somerset, England: Haynes Publishing, 2011.

Hough, David L. *Proficient Motorcycling: The Ultimate Guide to Riding Well.* Irvine, CA: BowTie Press, 2008.

Jonnum, Chris. *Museo Ducati: Six Decades of Classic Motorcycles of the Official Ducati Museum.* Phoenix, AZ: David Bull Publishing, 2012.

Klancher, Lee. *Motorcycle Dream Garages.* Minneapolis, MN: Motorbooks, 2009.

Lewis, Jack. *Coming and Going on Bikes: Essaying the Motorcycle.* Seattle, WA: Litsam, Inc., 2010.

Masi, C. G. *How to Set Up Your Motorcycle Workshop: Tips and Tricks for Building and Equipping Your Dream Workshop.* Center Conway, NH: Whitehorse Press, 2010.

McKechnie, Gary. *Great American Motorcycle Tours.* Berkeley, CA: Avalon Travel Publishing, 2006.

Pirsig, Robert M. *Zen and the Art of Motorcycle Maintenance: An Inquiry into Values.* New York, NY: William Morrow Paperbacks, 2008.

Walker, Mick. *Motorcycle: Evolution, Design, Passion.* Baltimore, MD: The Johns Hopkins University Press, 2006.

# BIBLIOGRAPHY

Ash, Kevin. "Ducati Diavel Review." *Telegraph*, February 14, 2012. Retrieved December 2012 (http://www.telegraph.co.uk/motoring/motorcycle_manufacturers/ducati/8314384/Ducati-Diavel-review.html).

Ash, Kevin. "Ducati Hypermotard 796 Review." *Telegraph*, October 30, 2009. Retrieved December 2012 (http://www.telegraph.co.uk/motoring/motorbikes/6460712/Ducati-Hypermotard-796-review.html).

Ash, Kevin. "Ducati Monster 796 Review." Ash on Bikes. Retrieved December 27, 2012 (http://www.ashonbikes.com/content/ducati-monster-796-review).

Ash, Kevin. "Ducati Streetfighter 848 Review." *Telegraph*, October 10, 2011. Retrieved December 2012 (http://www.telegraph.co.uk/motoring/motorcycle_manufacturers/ducati/8808940/Ducati-Streetfighter-848-review.html).

Beeler, Jensen. "Ride Review: Ducati Streetfighter 848." Asphalt & Rubber, April 6, 2012. Retrieved December 2012 (http://www.asphaltandrubber.com/reviews/ducati-streetfighter-848).

Callan, Kelly. "Ducati Monster 796: Review." Ultimate Motorcycling, October 13, 2012. Retrieved December 2012 (http://www.ultimatemotorcycling.com/2013-ducati-monster-796-review).

Cycle World. "Best Bikes of 2012." August 27, 2012. Retrieved December 2012 (http://www.cycleworld.com/2012/08/27/best-cruiser-ducati-diavel-carbon).

Ducati Monster Site. "Bike Details." Retrieved December 27, 2012 (http://www.monster.ducati.com/en/bike).

Ducati USA. Retrieved December 2012 and January 2013
(http://www.ducatiusa.com).

Duke, Kevin. "2012 Ducati 1199 Review." Motorcycle.com,
February 20, 2012. Retrieved December 2012 (http://www
.motorcycle.com/manufacturer/ducati/2012-ducati-1199
-panigale-review-video-91235.html).

Roderick, Tom. "2012 Ducati Chromo Review." Motorcycle.com,
August 12, 2012. Retrieved December 2012 (http://www
.motorcycle.com/manufacturer/ducati/2012-ducati-diavel
-cromo-review-91361.html).

Serafim. "2013 Ducati Hypermotard." TopSpeed.com, November
14, 2012. Retrieved December 2012 (http://www.topspeed
.com/motorcycles/motorcycle-reviews/ducati/2013-ducati
-hypermotard-ar137963.html).

Siahaan, Troy. "Top 10 Hottest Bikes of 2012," Motorcycle
.com, January 5, 2012. Retrieved December 2012 (http://
www.motorcycle.com/manufacturer/ducati/top-10-hottest
-bikes-of-2012-91201.html?page=3).

Siahaan, Troy. "2012 Ducati 1199 Panigale Preview."
Motorcycle.com, September 29, 2011. Retrieved
December 2012 (http://www.motorcycle.com/manufacturer
/ducati/2012-ducati-1199-panigale-preview-91138.html).

WorldSBK.com. "2012 Standings—FIM Superbike World
Championship." Retrieved December 28, 2012 (http://
www.worldsbk.com/en/season/standings.html).

# INDEX

# About the Author

Richard Barrington is an avid motorcyclist with nearly two decades of riding experience. His favorite rides are in the Finger Lakes region of New York State. When not riding motorcycles he is a senior financial analyst for MoneyRates.com. His articles have been syndicated on MSN.com, the *Huffington Post*, and Forbes.com, and he has appeared on National Public Radio's *Talk of the Nation* and American Public Media's *Marketplace*. He graduated from St. John Fisher College with a B.A. in communications and earned his Chartered Financial Analyst designation from the CFA Institute.

# Photo Credits

Cover, pp. 1, 4–5 Natursports/Shutterstock.com; pp. 8, 12 Thesupermat/Wikimedia Commons/File: Paris – Salon de la moto 2011 - Ducati – Diavel Cromo/CC BY-SA 3.0; p. 10 Bloomberg/Getty Images; p. 14 Kiyoshi Ota/Getty Images; p. 16 Thomas Schneider/imagebroker.net/SuperStock; p. 18 Rich Niewiroski Jr./Wikimedia Commons/File: 2007DucatiHyperMotard-001.jpg/CC BY 2.5; p. 20 Adriano Castelli/Shutterstock.com; p. 22 Franco Origlia/Getty Images; pp. 23, 32 Fast Bikes Magazine/Future/Getty Images; p. 26 Thesupermat/Wikimedia Commons/File: Paris – Salon de la moto 2011 - Ducati – Multistrada 1200 – 001.jpg/CC BY-SA 3.0; p. 29 imagebroker.net/SuperStock; p. 34 Thesupermat/Wikimedia Commons/File: Paris – Salon de la moto 2011 - Ducati – Streetfighter 848 – 003.jpg/CC BY-SA 3.0; p. 37 Pier Marco Tacca/Getty Images; p. 39 Desmodromico/Wikimedia Commons/File: Ducati 1199 Panigale engine2.jpg/CC BY-SA 3.0; interior pages background elements Dudarev Mikhail/Shutterstock.com, Yuriy_fx/Shutterstock.com; back cover © iStockphoto.com/JordiDelgado.

Designer: Brian Garvey; Editor: Nicholas Croce;
Photo Researcher: Karen Huang